Tech-Driven  Disease Detection

AI, Biomarkers, and Breakthrough Innovations Saving Lives

Taylor Royce

DEDICATION

To the unrelenting forerunners in medical innovation scientists, researchers, and medical professionals who push the envelope of what is possible in order to build a future in which early diagnosis saves lives.

To the patients and their families, whose fortitude and optimism fuel the demand for improved diagnostics and easily accessible medical care.

To the advocates, legislators, and educators who put in endless effort to close the gap between cutting-edge technology and practical applications.

And this book is for people who think that a world free of late-stage diagnosis is achievable.

DISCLAIMER

This book is meant solely for educational and informational purposes. It is not a diagnosis, treatment, or medical advice, nor is it a replacement for expert medical counsel. Regarding any medical concerns, symptoms, or treatment choices, readers are urged to speak with licensed healthcare providers.

Although every attempt has been made to guarantee the correctness and dependability of the data provided, medical technology and research are always changing. The completeness, accuracy, and applicability of the information in this book are not guaranteed by the author or publisher, either explicitly or implicitly.

Additionally, explanations of breakthroughs in genetics, artificial intelligence, medical technology, diagnostic tools, and other fields are grounded in the most recent knowledge available at the time of writing. For the most recent information, readers should consult official regulatory authorities and professional associations as clinical applications, regulatory approvals, and healthcare policies are subject to change over time.

Any loss, harm, or damage resulting from the use or abuse of the information contained in this book is not covered by the publisher or author. The reader is free to rely on any information presented here at their own risk.

CONTENTS

ACKNOWLEDGMENTS

Without the wonderful assistance, wisdom, and encouragement of numerous people and organizations, the writing of this book would not have been possible.

Above all, I want to express my sincere gratitude to the doctors, scientists, and inventors whose commitment to improving early disease detection is influencing healthcare today and in the future. Much of what is covered in this book is based on their innovative work in personalized medicine, genetics, nanotechnology, and artificial intelligence.

The developers, engineers, and scientists who are pushing the limits of diagnostic technology have my sincere gratitude as well. Their unrelenting quest for creativity has produced ground-breaking ideas that could save countless lives.

To my mentors, and coworkers: your insightful conversations, helpful criticism, and enthusiasm for medical progress have been vital during this journey. Your viewpoints have enhanced this study and helped me better grasp the opportunities and difficulties associated with early disease diagnosis.

I express my gratitude to my family and friends for their consistent encouragement, patience, and support. Even at the most trying times, your faith in my vision kept me going.

Finally, I would like to thank all of the readers for their curiosity and dedication to learning, regardless of whether they are researchers, policymakers, healthcare professionals, or anyone else interested in the future of diagnostics. I sincerely hope that this book offers insightful information and stimulates more conversations on how to make healthcare better for everyone.

CHAPTER 1

THE VALUE OF EARLY DISEASE DETECTION

Over time, disease detection has drastically changed, moving from reactive treatment methods to proactive and preventive care. A key component of contemporary medicine is early disease identification, which enables prompt intervention, higher survival rates, and lower medical expenses. This chapter will address the importance of early detection, look at case studies showing how it can save lives, talk about the difficulties with conventional diagnostic techniques, and assess how technology can help with early diagnosis.

1.1 Knowing How Disease Develops: The Importance of Early Detection

Diseases progress over time, especially chronic and life-threatening ailments including cancer, heart disease, and neurological problems. Many often, symptoms don't show up until the illness has progressed considerably, which reduces the effectiveness of treatment and the likelihood of positive results. Knowing how illnesses develop helps explain why early detection is so important.

Disease Progression Stages

The majority of illnesses develop in phases:

- Initiation Phase: During this phase, molecular or cellular alterations start but are not observable using standard techniques. At this point, genetic predispositions, inflammation, or mutations begin to impact how the body functions.

- Latent or Asymptomatic Phase: The illness is present but has not yet shown any discernible signs. For instance, tumors are still too small to be seen with conventional imaging, even if malignant cells may proliferate.

- Phase of Early Manifestation: There may be mild or nebulous symptoms that are frequently confused with minor medical conditions. For example, early symptoms of conditions like Alzheimer's may be written off as mere forgetfulness.

- Advanced Disease Phase: The illness manifests all of

its symptoms, frequently with dire repercussions. Lower survival rates result from more difficult and ineffective treatment at this point.

Early disease detection is essential for the following reasons:

- With lifestyle changes and focused interventions, the disease may be stopped or even reversed. Treatment is frequently easier, less invasive, and more effective.
- By avoiding costly late-stage therapies, healthcare expenses can be drastically decreased.

1.2 The Potential for Life-Saving Early Diagnosis: Examples in Cancer and Other Conditions

It has been demonstrated that early diagnosis can save lives, especially in cases of diabetes, heart disease, and cancer. Several studies demonstrate how early identification raises quality of life and survival rates.

Case Study: Identification of Cancer

One of the most important diseases where early identification has a major impact is cancer. Think about ovarian cancer:

- The five-year survival rate for ovarian cancer is 93% if it is discovered at a localized stage. However, survival rates drop to 30% or less when the disease is discovered in its advanced stages.
- Screening Advances: Early detection is now feasible thanks to imaging methods like transvaginal ultrasounds and blood tests that identify indicators like CA-125.

In a similar vein, the survival rate for melanoma, a very deadly type of skin cancer, is 32% once the cancer spreads, compared to 99% when detected early.

Case Study: Heart Conditions

Unnoticed warning signals are common for cardiac illnesses, including heart attacks and strokes. Early diagnosis is made possible by technologies such as wearable cardiac monitors and coronary calcium scoring, which lower the likelihood of deadly cardiovascular events.

Neurodegenerative Diseases Case Study

Although early diagnosis of Alzheimer's disease is notoriously challenging, new developments in AI-driven cognitive testing and blood tests for beta-amyloid proteins give hope for earlier treatments.

These case studies show that treatment success rates soar, patient outcomes improve, and total healthcare burdens reduce when diseases are identified before they completely appear.

1.3 Traditional Diagnosis Challenges: The Reasons Many Illnesses Are Not Identified Until It's Too Late

Even though early detection has many advantages, standard diagnostic techniques have a number of drawbacks that cause diagnosis to be delayed.

No Initial Symptoms

In their early stages, many diseases, such as hypertension and pancreatic cancer, may not show any discernible symptoms. Patients may put off being checked out until it's too late because they feel completely well.

Ineffective Screening Techniques

Conventional screening methods frequently use antiquated or vague indicators. For instance:

- Although mammograms are a useful tool for identifying breast cancer, they can occasionally provide false positives or negative results.
- Diabetic blood sugar tests might not detect prediabetes in time to stop its progression.

Restricted Healthcare Access

Obtaining early diagnostic tools is still difficult in many regions of the world. The infrastructure necessary for routine examinations is frequently lacking in underserved areas, low-income neighborhoods, and rural areas.

The delayed interpretation and incorrect diagnosis

Misdiagnosis is still a widespread problem, even in cases where symptoms are apparent. For example:

- Multiple sclerosis in its early stages might be confused with migraines.

- Indigestion is frequently blamed for pancreatic cancer symptoms including minor abdominal pain.

These difficulties highlight how urgently diagnostic technology must progress in order to guarantee that illnesses are identified in time for efficient treatment.

1.4 Technology's Contribution to Closing the Diagnostic Divide

By improving diagnostics' speed, accuracy, and accessibility, emerging technologies are revolutionizing the identification of disease. These developments, which range from biomarker-based testing to artificial intelligence, have the potential to completely transform early detection.

Early Detection with Artificial Intelligence

Large volumes of data can be analyzed by AI-powered diagnostic systems, which can then spot trends that human physicians might overlook. Among the significant advancements are:

- AI-assisted Radiology: Highly accurate tumor, fracture, and abnormality detection is possible thanks to algorithms trained on thousands of medical pictures.
- In order to forecast disease risk years in advance, AI models use lifestyle and genetic data.

Liquid biopsies and biomarkers

Biological substances known as biomarkers are used to detect the presence of disease. Contemporary biomarker-based assays, including liquid biopsies, enable:

- Non-invasive Cancer Detection: Blood samples can be used to identify circulating tumor DNA (ctDNA), which offers early cancer detection before the disease spreads.
- Neurological Disease Monitoring: A potential advance in early diagnosis is provided by blood tests for proteins specific to Alzheimer's disease.

Remote and Wearable Health Monitoring

Smartwatches and continuous glucose monitors are

examples of wearable technology that offers real-time health insights to help diagnose diseases early. These consist of:

- Atrial fibrillation can be detected by ECG-enabled wearables before symptoms appear.
- Continuous glucose monitors that detect patterns of prediabetes before diabetes becomes a serious condition.

Nanotechnology in the Identification of Diseases

Nanotechnology developments have made it possible to create extremely sensitive diagnostic instruments, such as:

- Devices that use phase imaging technology to identify cancer markers or infections in blood and saliva samples are known as smartphone-based diagnostics.
- Lab-on-a-chip technologies: tiny lab equipment capable of immediately analyzing tiny blood samples for illness indicators.

More diseases are being detected in their early stages

thanks to these advancements, which are quickly reducing the time between symptom development and diagnosis.

A key element of contemporary healthcare is early disease identification, which greatly enhances patient outcomes and lowers healthcare costs. Knowing how a disease develops emphasizes the importance of early intervention. Case studies from the real world in cancer, heart disease, and neurological illnesses demonstrate how early detection can save lives. Traditional diagnostic techniques, however, include drawbacks such misdiagnosis, delayed symptom manifestation, and restricted access to medical care.

Early detection is changing as a result of technological developments including artificial intelligence (AI), biomarker-based testing, wearable health monitoring, and nanotechnology. These developments have the potential to completely transform preventative medicine as they develop further, giving more people access to prompt diagnosis and efficient care. Proactive disease identification is the key to the future of healthcare, ultimately saving millions of lives.

CHAPTER 2

EARLY DIAGNOSIS WITH AI AND MACHINE LEARNING

Early disease detection is being revolutionized by artificial intelligence (AI) and machine learning (ML), which increase diagnostic accuracy, speed up results, and decrease human error. AI-driven technologies are being used more and more to evaluate genetic markers, spot trends in medical imaging, and forecast the start of diseases before symptoms show up, all thanks to the exponential growth of healthcare data.

The process of training AI models for medical diagnosis, practical applications in domains like neurology and oncology, the ethical and legal issues surrounding the use of AI in healthcare, and how AI is changing disease detection are all covered in this chapter.

2.1 An Overview of How AI Is Revolutionizing Disease Detection

Results from traditional diagnostic techniques can vary since they frequently rely on human judgment, laborious testing, and subjective evaluations. This landscape is being altered by AI by:

- Improving Diagnostic Accuracy: AI-driven systems are able to analyze enormous volumes of medical data and identify trends that human doctors would miss.

- Speeding Up Diagnosis: AI systems can evaluate genetic sequences, lab results, and medical scans in a matter of seconds, cutting down on the time it takes to identify diseases.

- Reducing Human Error: AI algorithms that have been trained on large datasets are more accurate than conventional techniques at spotting early disease symptoms.

- Personalizing Treatment Plans: By detecting distinct illness signs in each patient, AI-driven diagnostics enable more specialized treatments.

Primary AI Tools for Illness Identification

1. Deep Learning: A branch of artificial intelligence that analyzes medical images using neural networks to identify anomalies like tumors or fractures.

2. Natural Language Processing (NLP): AI systems that use patient histories to search electronic health records (EHRs) for early illness warning indicators.

3. In order to enable early interventions, predictive analytics: AI models evaluate a patient's risk variables by examining genetic, lifestyle, and medical data.

4. Computer Vision: AI-powered image recognition systems that assist radiologists in finding anomalies in X-rays, MRIs, and CT scans.

AI is becoming a vital weapon in the fight against deadly illnesses as a result of these developments, which are changing healthcare from reactive to preventive care.

2.2 Accuracy, Data, and Algorithms in Training AI Models for Medical Diagnosis

The accuracy of predictions, the resilience of algorithms, and the quality of data all affect how well AI performs in early diagnosis.

Data: The Basis of Healthcare AI

Large datasets are necessary for AI models to learn from, including:

- Medical Imaging Datasets: AI is trained on MRI, CT, and X-ray images to identify anomalies.
- AI can identify illness trends with the use of clinical notes, test findings, and patient histories found in electronic health records, or EHRs.
- DNA sequencing data that allows AI to identify genetic susceptibilities to diseases is known as "genomic and biomarker data."

To avoid inequities in AI-driven diagnoses, the difficulty is in making sure that these datasets are thorough, objective, and varied.

AI Diagnostics: Powered by Algorithms

AI models process medical data using complex algorithms. Several popular methods include:

- Convolutional neural networks, or CNNs, are used in image processing to identify abnormalities in organs, fractures, and cancers.
- Recurrent neural networks, or RNNs, are used in natural language processing (NLP) to glean valuable information from clinical notes and patient data.
- Decision trees and random forests are machine learning algorithms that forecast the likelihood of a disease based on a variety of patient characteristics.

Before being used in clinical settings, these algorithms undergo extensive testing on a variety of datasets to guarantee their dependability.

Verification and Accuracy

For AI-based diagnostic tools to be used in medical

practice, they must adhere to strict accuracy requirements. Validation is accomplished by:

- Radiologists', pathologists', and doctors' diagnoses are contrasted with AI predictions in a process known as "cross-validation with human experts."
- Clinical Trials: AI models undergo extensive testing before they may be employed in hospitals and research facilities.
- Regulatory Approval: Before being used in clinical settings, AI technologies must adhere to regulations established by healthcare regulators like the FDA and EMA.

Even with these developments, there are still issues with making sure AI models are objective, understandable, and updated often to reflect new medical research.

2.3 Practical Uses: AI for Neurological Conditions, Cancer Screening, and More

AI is already being utilized to enhance early detection in a number of medical specialties. Among the most important applications are:

Using AI to Detect Cancer

- AI-powered mammography interpretation has reduced false positives and negatives and increased early detection rates for breast cancer.
- In order to increase survival rates, deep learning algorithms examine CT scans to identify lung nodules before symptoms manifest.
- Colorectal Cancer: Compared to manual methods, AI-assisted colonoscopy instruments help detect polyps and abnormal growths more precisely.

AI in Diagnosing Neurological Diseases

- Alzheimer's Disease: AI-powered brain imaging analysis facilitates early intervention by identifying structural alterations associated with early-stage Alzheimer's.
- Parkinson's Disease: AI-driven movement monitoring and voice analysis identify early indicators of Parkinson's before motor symptoms

worsen.

- Stroke Prediction: AI algorithms evaluate imaging and patient history to determine the risk of stroke, enabling preventive actions.

Cardiology and AI

- ECG Interpretation: AI improves the analysis of electrocardiograms (ECGs), accurately identifying heart irregularities and arrhythmias.
- Heart Failure Prediction: Using biomarkers and clinical data, predictive analytics determine whether people are at risk of heart failure.

AI in the Monitoring of Infectious Diseases

- COVID-19 Detection: AI-powered analysis of chest X-rays helps identify COVID-19 infections, increasing the effectiveness of triage.
- In order to assist fight antibiotic resistance, artificial intelligence (AI) examines bacterial genomes to forecast resistance tendencies.

These uses show how AI is changing current medicine, enhancing patient outcomes, and filling gaps in early detection.

2.4 The Legal and Ethical Environment of AI in Healthcare

Even though AI has great promise for early disease identification, responsible deployment requires attention to ethical and regulatory issues.

Ethical Issues

1. Bias in AI Models: AI algorithms may generate biased findings that disproportionately impact particular groups if training data is not varied.
2. Data Privacy and Security: Because AI uses enormous volumes of patient data, there are worries about data breaches and illegal access.
3. In order for physicians and patients to comprehend the rationale behind a diagnosis, AI judgments must be explicable. This is known as algorithm transparency.

Regulatory Difficulties

1. FDA and EMA Approval: To guarantee that AI-driven medical software and devices fulfill safety and efficacy requirements, they must go through extensive testing.
2. HIPAA and GDPR Compliance: To secure patient data, AI systems must abide by data protection regulations.
3. Integration into Clinical Workflows: AI must be carefully incorporated into current healthcare systems in order to support medical practitioners rather than replace them.

Overcoming the Obstacles

- Creating Ethical AI Guidelines: To reduce biases and improve equity in AI applications, standardized rules ought to be implemented.
- Improving Data Security Measures: Decentralized data storage and encryption can help safeguard patient data.

- Improving AI Interpretability: Explainable AI (XAI) research guarantees that human specialists can verify machine-generated diagnoses.

AI can be safely incorporated into healthcare by resolving these moral and legal concerns, optimizing its potential while lowering dangers.

Early disease identification is being revolutionized by AI and machine learning, which is also increasing accuracy, decreasing diagnostic delays, and facilitating individualized treatments. AI-driven technologies are increasing the effectiveness of early detection in a variety of medical domains by utilizing deep learning, natural language processing, and predictive analytics.

However, reliable algorithms, rigorous validation procedures, and high-quality data are necessary for AI to succeed in the healthcare industry. Although practical uses in neurology, cardiology, and cancer show AI's potential to save lives, ethical and legal issues need to be properly handled.

A new era of precision medicine and proactive healthcare will be ushered in as AI's involvement in early disease identification grows. AI has the potential to close important diagnostic gaps and enhance patient outcomes globally if it is implemented responsibly.

CHAPTER 3

BIOMARKER TESTING AND LIQUID BIOPSY

A revolutionary method for detecting diseases, especially in oncology, is liquid biopsy. By identifying disease-related biomarkers in physiological fluids like blood, urine, and saliva, liquid biopsy provides a non-invasive alternative to standard tissue biopsies, which require invasive surgical procedures to obtain a sample for examination. Personalized medicine, therapy monitoring, and early diagnosis could all be transformed by this approach.

The basics of liquid biopsy, the function of biomarkers in early disease detection, a case study of Biological Dynamics' lab-on-a-chip test for pancreatic cancer, and the potential for liquid biopsy to eventually replace conventional biopsy techniques are all covered in this chapter.

3.1 Liquid Biopsy: What Is It? Comprehending the Identification of Blood-Based Diseases

A diagnostic method called liquid biopsy examines blood components in circulation to identify illnesses like cancer early on. These elements could consist of proteins, extracellular vesicles (EVs), circulating tumor cells (CTCs), and circulating tumor DNA (ctDNA).

The Operation of Liquid Biopsy

Advanced molecular biology techniques are used in liquid biopsies to identify and examine disease-related biomarkers in bodily fluids. The following steps are typically included in the process:

1. Sample Collection: The patient has a tiny amount of blood (or another fluid) extracted.
2. Biomarker Isolation: CtDNA, CTCs, or other biomarkers are extracted from the material by processing.
3. Genetic and Molecular Analysis: To find mutations, gene expressions, or other disease markers,

high-throughput sequencing or other molecular approaches are employed.

4. Clinical Interpretation: The findings are examined to ascertain the existence, course, or reaction to therapy of the disease.

Liquid Biopsy Benefits

- Non-Invasive: Liquid biopsies just require a basic blood sample, as opposed to standard biopsies that necessitate tissue extraction.

- Early detection allows for earlier intervention by identifying illness signs prior to the onset of symptoms.

- Real-Time Monitoring: Enables ongoing monitoring of the course of the disease and the effectiveness of treatment.

- Compared to a single tissue biopsy sample, a comprehensive analysis offers a more comprehensive view of tumor heterogeneity.

Restrictions and Difficulties

Despite its benefits, liquid biopsy has a number of drawbacks.

- Some liquid biopsy tests may have trouble detecting very low quantities of biomarkers, which could result in misleading negative results.
- Standardization Issues: Reproducibility and dependability are impacted by the absence of uniform techniques among laboratories.
- Regulatory Obstacles: Before being widely used in clinical settings, liquid biopsy technologies need to pass stringent validation.

3.2 The Secret to Early Cancer and Other Disease Detection: Biomarkers

Biomarkers are quantifiable biological substances that show whether a physiological process is normal or abnormal. Biomarkers are essential for detecting illnesses early on in liquid biopsies.

Liquid Biopsy Biomarker Types

1. Circulating Tumor DNA (ctDNA): DNA fragments released into the bloodstream by tumor cells.

- Utilized to identify mutations and provide focused treatments.
- Able to detect resistance mutations and monitor therapy response.

2. The second type of cancer cells that separate from the main tumor and enter the bloodstream are called circulating tumor cells, or CTCs.

- Give information about the biology of tumors and their potential for metastasis.
- Assist with prognosis and individualized treatment schedules.

3. Cells generate tiny vesicles called extracellular vesicles (EVs), which transport substances such as proteins and RNA.

- Contribute to the development of disease and intercellular communication.
- Potential application in the diagnosis of cancer and neurological illnesses.

4. Protein Biomarkers: Blood samples can reveal proteins linked to particular illnesses.

- Examples are CA-125 for ovarian cancer and

prostate-specific antigen (PSA) for prostate cancer.

Biomarker Applications in Disease Detection

- **Cancer Diagnosis and Monitoring:** Biomarkers aid in the identification of tumor progression and genetic alterations.
- Neurodegenerative Disorders: Blood tests can detect biomarkers for Alzheimer's disease, such as tau proteins.
- Detection of Infectious Diseases: Biomarker-based testing is able to identify illnesses like tuberculosis and hepatitis before symptoms show up.
- Prediction of Cardiovascular Disease: Blood biomarkers can determine the likelihood of strokes or heart attacks.

3.3 Case Study: Lab-on-a-Chip Testing for Pancreatic Cancer and Biological Dynamics

The lab-on-a-chip technique developed by Biological Dynamics, which attempts to enhance early detection of pancreatic cancer, is one of the most promising advancements in liquid biopsy.

The Pancreatic Cancer Detection Challenge

Because there are no obvious signs and no effective screening techniques, pancreatic cancer is notoriously hard to detect early. The disease has frequently proceeded to an incurable state by the time it is discovered.

Lab-on-a-Chip Solution from Biological Dynamics

A microfluidic lab-on-a-chip device created by the biotechnology business Biological Dynamics makes it possible to quickly and extremely sensitively identify pancreatic cancer biomarkers.

Lab-on-a-Chip Operation

1. Microfluidic Separation: The apparatus separates extracellular vesicles containing biomarkers linked to cancer from blood samples using electric fields.
2. Molecular Analysis: Protein expressions and genetic mutations associated with pancreatic cancer are

examined in the retrieved vesicles.

3. Quick Outcomes: When compared to conventional laboratory techniques, the approach drastically cuts down on the amount of time needed for biomarker detection.

Clinical Effects and Possible Advantages

- Earlier Detection: Survival rates are increased when cancer is detected early.
- Minimally Invasive: Complex biopsy procedures are replaced with a straightforward blood test.
- Scalability: The technology's use is not limited to oncology; it can be modified to identify biomarkers for various illnesses.

This case study demonstrates how important issues in early disease diagnosis are being addressed by technological advancements in liquid biopsy.

3.4 Prospects for the Future: How Liquid Biopsy May Take the Place of Conventional Biopsy

It is anticipated that liquid biopsies will become more common in healthcare and may eventually take the place of traditional tissue biopsies in many clinical situations.

New Developments Fueling Adoption of Liquid Biopsies

1. Enhanced Sensitivity and Specificity: Detection methods are being improved through ongoing research to reduce false positives and false negatives.

2. Incorporation of AI and Machine Learning: State-of-the-art computer models can improve biomarker analysis and yield more precise illness forecasts.

3. Cost Reduction: Liquid biopsy testing will become more widely available and less expensive as technologies advance.

4. Breader Disease Applications: Research is extending the use of liquid biopsy beyond the diagnosis of cancer to ailments like autoimmune disorders, Alzheimer's, and cardiovascular diseases.

A Chance to Take the Place of Conventional Biopsies

Although liquid biopsy has a lot of potential, it won't be able to fully replace standard biopsy anytime soon. It is necessary to address a number of factors:

- Tissue-Specific Analysis: For a conclusive diagnosis, tissue investigation is still necessary for certain disorders.
- Standardization and Regulatory Approval: Global clinical validation is necessary for widespread adoption.
- Healthcare Integration: To properly interpret the results of liquid biopsies, medical personnel require training.

The Future Vision

With further development, liquid biopsy may replace traditional biopsy as a common diagnostic technique because it is quicker, less intrusive, and more efficient. It has the potential to revolutionize precision medicine by facilitating earlier diagnosis and more individualized treatment plans for a variety of illnesses.

A major advancement in customized medicine and early disease detection is represented by liquid biopsy. It provides a less intrusive option to conventional tissue biopsy by utilizing biomarkers such ctDNA, CTCs, and extracellular vesicles. Advances in cancer diagnosis are being accelerated by technologies such as the lab-on-a-chip, which shows how liquid biopsy might enhance patient outcomes.

Liquid biopsy has the potential to completely transform healthcare as long as research keeps improving its precision, lowering costs, and broadening its uses. The future of illness detection is moving toward a more accurate, non-invasive, and accessible method, one that may ultimately completely change how we diagnose and treat diseases in the twenty-first century even though standardization and clinical validation still present difficulties.

CHAPTER 4

AT-HOME DIAGNOSTICS USING NANOTECHNOLOGY

Medical diagnostics is being revolutionized by nanotechnology, which makes it possible to do tests at home that are extremely sensitive, quick, and affordable. At-home diagnostics are becoming more widely available because of the combination of nanoscale materials, artificial intelligence, and smartphone-based analysis, enabling people to keep an eye on their health without going to a hospital.

The importance of nanotechnology in medical testing, the emergence of smartphone-based illness detection, the developments in phase imaging technology, and the prospects and problems of making nanotechnology-based diagnostics widely available are all covered in this chapter.

4.1 Nanotechnology's Function in Medical Testing

The manipulation of matter at the atomic or molecular scale, usually between 1 and 100 nanometers, is known as nanotechnology. Nanotechnology has made it possible to create extremely accurate instruments for early disease detection in the field of medical diagnostics.

How Medical Testing Is Improved by Nanotechnology

Medical testing is enhanced by nanotechnology in a number of ways:

1. Enhanced Sensitivity: Early diagnosis is made possible by nanoscale biosensors' ability to identify trace amounts of disease biomarkers.
2. Quick Results: When compared to conventional laboratory testing, nano-based tests can provide results in a matter of minutes, cutting down on wait times.
3. Non-Invasive Techniques: A lot of diagnostics based on nanotechnology employ blood, urine, or saliva from a simple finger prick, doing away with the necessity for uncomfortable procedures.
4. Lower Costs: Nanotechnology can lower the cost

and increase the accessibility of diagnostics by streamlining intricate testing processes.

5. Portability: Due to their tiny size, nano-based diagnostic tools can be included into smartphone or handheld systems for usage at home.

Nanotechnology's Principal Use in Diagnostics

- Early detection of cancer biomarkers in blood, urine, or saliva is possible with nanoparticles.

- The ability of nano-based sensors to swiftly identify bacteria and viruses helps in the prompt identification of illnesses including HIV, TB, and COVID-19.

- Diabetes Monitoring: Continuous sensors made possible by nanotechnology enable more precise glucose monitoring.

- Neurological Disease Screening: Nanomaterial-based biomarker detection for early Alzheimer's and Parkinson's disease identification.

4.2 Disease Detection via Smartphone: The Operation of Nano-Devices

At-home diagnostics is being revolutionized by the combination of smartphones and nanotechnology, which enables people to do sophisticated medical tests with only a portable gadget. This invention uses cloud-based connection, AI-powered data processing, and nanosensors to provide customers with medical-grade testing.

The Operation of Nano-Devices Based on Smartphones

1. Sample Collection: Users supply a biological sample, such as blood from a tiny finger prick, urine, or saliva.

2. Nanosensor Analysis: A nano-based biosensor that interacts with the sample to identify particular disease biomarkers.

3. Smartphone Processing: The reaction is analyzed and the outcomes are interpreted by the smartphone's camera, microfluidic chip, or external sensor.

4. Cloud-Based AI Interpretation: Sophisticated algorithms provide an accurate diagnosis by

comparing the results with medical databases.

5. Real-Time Feedback: The results are shown promptly on the smartphone app, which also offers suggestions, including seeing a doctor if necessary.

Instances of Nanotechnology Diagnostics Using Smartphones

- COVID-19 Testing: Rapid at-home results are provided using mobile nano-sensors that have been created to identify viral particles in saliva samples.

- Glucose Monitoring for Diabetics: Nanosensors built into smartphones continuously detect blood or sweat glucose levels, eliminating the need for repeated finger pricks.

- Urinalysis for Kidney and Liver Health: Test strips with nanosensors integrated into them analyze urine samples and deliver immediate findings through a mobile app.

- Detection of Skin Cancer: AI-enabled smartphone cameras in conjunction with imaging based on nanotechnology can examine skin lesions for early indications of melanoma.

Users may now conveniently track their health from home thanks to the integration of cellphones and nanotechnology, which is making diagnostics more accessible.

4.3 Phase Imaging Technology: A New Development in At-Home Diagnosis

Without the use of dyes or staining agents, phase imaging technology is a new diagnostic technique that improves the visualization of biological materials. Phase imaging enables more accurate at-home medical diagnostics when paired with nanotechnology.

Phase Imaging Technology: What Is It?

The process of measuring the phase shift of light as it travels through transparent biological materials, such tissues, bacteria, or blood cells, is known as phase imaging. Phase imaging offers a more thorough, real-time study than classical microscopy, which uses chemical staining to see materials.

How Phase Imaging Improves Diagnostics at Home

1. Label-Free Testing: Removes the requirement for staining agents, which simplifies and secures testing for use at home.

2. Early illness diagnosis is made possible by High-Resolution Imaging: which picks up on minute cellular alterations.

3. Real-Time Analysis: Offers immediate diagnostic feedback without the need for processing in a lab.

4. Integration with Smartphones: Capable of being reduced in size to consumer-use portable devices.

Phase imaging applications in at-home diagnostics

- Blood Cell Analysis: Blood samples can be analyzed by users to identify infections, anemia, and other illnesses.

- Urine Microscopy: By analyzing urine samples, phase imaging can detect indicators of kidney illness.

- The ability to quickly identify pathogens in bodily fluids is made possible by bacterial and viral infections.

- Cancer Screening: By examining their distinct optical characteristics, early-stage cancer cells can be recognized.

It is anticipated that phase imaging technology combined with nanotechnology would improve at-home diagnostic capabilities even further as it develops.

4.4 Difficulties and Possibilities: Making Nanotech Diagnostics Accessible to All

Nanotechnology holds potential for at-home diagnostics, but a number of obstacles must be overcome before it can be extensively used. Ongoing developments, however, offer promising prospects for the future.

Difficulties with Broad Adoption

1. Regulatory Approval: Diagnostic instruments based on nanotechnology need to pass stringent testing and receive FDA and EMA approval.
2. Manufacturing Scalability: One of the biggest

challenges is producing nano-based diagnostic kits in large quantities while keeping them reasonably priced.

3. Data Privacy Concerns: It is crucial to safeguard patient data from cybersecurity risks as diagnostics grow more digital and cloud-connected.

4. User Education: To properly use diagnostic equipment based on nanotechnology and understand data, consumers require the right advice.

5. Integration with Healthcare Systems: To integrate nanotechnology diagnostics into routine medical procedures, physicians and other healthcare workers need to receive training.

Future Prospects and Opportunities

1. Advances in AI and Machine Learning: AI-powered diagnostics can offer real-time health insights and increase accuracy.

2. Lower Costs Through Mass Production: Advances in the production of nanomaterials will reduce the cost of at-home diagnostics.

3. Telemedicine Integration: By improving remote

patient monitoring, nano-based diagnostics enable physicians to evaluate patients without in-person visits.

4. Expanded Disease Coverage: As nanotechnology advances, more diseases, such as autoimmune disorders and cardiovascular ailments, will have diagnostic tools developed.

5. Global Health Impact: Advanced medical testing can be introduced to underprivileged areas of the world using portable, reasonably priced nanotechnology diagnostics.

The field of at-home diagnostics is changing due to nanotechnology, which promises a time when people will be able to easily and precisely monitor their health. These developments, which range from phase imaging technology to smartphone-based disease detection, are increasing the accessibility and convenience of early diagnosis.

Although issues like user education, data security, and regulatory approval need to be resolved, the advantages of nanotechnology in diagnostics greatly exceed these drawbacks. Nanotechnology has the potential to completely transform personal healthcare, enabling people to take charge of their health from the comfort of their own homes as long as research and development efforts keep pushing the envelope.

CHAPTER 5

MONITORING DISEASES WITH WEARABLE HEALTH TECHNOLOGY

The way that people and medical professionals track, identify, and treat illnesses is being completely transformed by wearable health technology. Wearables are evolving from fitness trackers to advanced medical devices with real-time illness monitoring capabilities because of developments in biosensors, artificial intelligence, and miniature electronics. Continuous data on critical health parameters is provided by these devices, allowing for the early detection of diseases like diabetes, heart disease, and even cancer risks.

This chapter examines the future of wearable health technology, the effects of wearables on healthcare, the value of real-time monitoring in illness prevention, and developments in non-invasive glucose and cardiovascular health tracking.

5.1 How Wearables Are Transforming Healthcare: From Smartwatches to Biosensors

From basic step counters to sophisticated biosensors that can identify intricate physiological changes, wearable health technology has improved significantly. These gadgets use state-of-the-art technology to track a number of health indicators, such as blood oxygen levels, glucose levels, heart rate, and even early indicators of neurological conditions.

Important Types of Wearable Medical Equipment

1. Fitness trackers and smartwatches: these devices are outfitted with sensors to gauge physical activity, blood oxygen levels, and heart rate. ECG (electrocardiogram) monitoring is available on some devices, such as the Fitbit and Apple Watch, to identify atrial fibrillation.

2. CGMs, or continuous glucose monitors

- Diabetics can monitor their blood sugar levels

without using finger pricks thanks to devices like the Freestyle Libre and Dexcom G6.

- Real-time glucose monitoring lowers the chance of both hyperglycemia and hypoglycemia.

3. Wearable ECG Monitors

- These portable devices measure cardiovascular stress, heart rate variability, and abnormal heart rhythms.
- Early identification of cardiac illness is accomplished by devices such as the KardiaMobile and Withings Move ECG.

4. Biosensor Patches

- Biochemical sensors embedded in thin, flexible patches measure skin temperature, perspiration, and other indicators.
- able to identify stress markers, lactate levels, and dehydration.

5. Smart Rings and Other Small Wearables

- Oura Ring and comparable gadgets monitor respiration rate, body temperature, and sleep habits.

- Used to diagnose diseases, such as COVID-19, early.

Cloud-Based Data Processing and AI's Expanding Role

- In order to assess health data in real-time, wearables are increasingly incorporating AI-driven algorithms.
- Doctors may remotely monitor patients and modify therapies depending on real-time information thanks to cloud connectivity.
- By identifying trends in their physiological readings, AI-powered insights assist users in interpreting their health data and provide lifestyle advice.

5.2 Live Heart Disease, Diabetes, and Cancer Risk Monitoring

Real-time disease monitoring is one of wearable health technology's biggest benefits. People may now continuously monitor their health rather than depending on sporadic exams, which enables early action before symptoms deteriorate.

Wearables for Heart Disease Monitoring

- Electrocardiogram (ECG) Monitoring: Atrial fibrillation, a significant risk factor for stroke, can be identified by smartwatches equipped with ECG sensors.
- Heart Rate Variability (HRV) Tracking: Tracks variations in heart rate, which might reveal cardiovascular problems and stress levels.
- Monitoring Blood Pressure: Cuffless blood pressure monitoring is currently a feature of advanced wearables, which helps people with hypertension control their condition.

Glucose monitoring and diabetes management

- By providing minute-by-minute glucose measurements, continuous glucose monitors (CGMs) lower the possibility of harmful variations.
- CGMs with AI capabilities examine patterns and offer nutritional and lifestyle advice.
- Certain wearables assess glucose non-invasively using perspiration or interstitial fluid, doing away with the requirement for needle-based testing.

Early Warning and Cancer Risk Detection Systems

- Skin Cancer Detection: Wearable skin sensors are able to detect abnormal moles or lesions by analyzing UV exposure.
- Breast Cancer Monitoring: Biosensor-equipped smart bras identify temperature changes in breast tissue, which could be a sign of tumor growth.
- AI-Powered Risk Assessment: By analyzing gathered health data, wearables offer early risk evaluations based on physiological indicators, genetic variables, and lifestyle choices.

By enabling people to manage their health proactively rather than waiting for symptoms to manifest, wearable technology is changing healthcare from reactive to preventative care.

5.3 Developments in Cardiovascular Health Monitoring and Non-Invasive Glucose Monitoring

The creation of non-invasive diagnostic instruments is one

of the most significant developments in wearable health technology. Blood samples or invasive procedures are frequently needed for traditional ways of evaluating cardiovascular health or glucose levels. Recent developments in biosensing technology, however, are making these procedures more accessible and pleasant.

Glucose Monitoring Without Invasion

Researchers have been working for years to create glucose monitoring tools that don't require finger pricks. The most recent developments consist of:

- **Optical Glucose Sensors:** Measure blood glucose levels through the skin using Raman or infrared spectroscopy.
- Without requiring blood samples, sweat-based glucose monitoring measures the amount of glucose in perspiration.
- Electromagnetic Sensors: Measure blood glucose levels without penetrating the skin by using radio waves.
- Intelligent contact lenses: These spectacles, created

by firms such as Google Verily, measure the amount of glucose in tears.

By making glucose monitoring easier and less painful, these technologies are completely changing the way people manage their diabetes.

Innovations in Cardiovascular Health Monitoring

- Cuffless Blood Pressure Monitors: Accurate blood pressure measurements are possible without an inflated cuff thanks to new wearable sensors.
- AI-Powered ECG Analysis: Sophisticated algorithms are able to identify heart murmurs, arrhythmias, and even the precursors of heart attacks.
- Blood Oxygen and Respiratory Rate Monitoring: SpO2 levels, which can be a sign of cardiovascular or respiratory problems, are measured by devices such as the Apple Watch.
- Early Stroke Detection: Wearables that can identify abrupt changes in blood pressure and irregular heartbeats can alert users to possible strokes before

they happen.

Wearable technology is helping to lower the death rate from heart disease, which is still the world's leading cause of death, by offering continuous cardiovascular monitoring.

5.4 Future Trends: Personalized Health Insights, Implantable Sensors, and Smart Fabrics

Researchers and businesses are creating increasingly sophisticated wearable health technology solutions that will blend in perfectly with daily living as it develops further.

Bio-Integrated Clothes and Smart Fabrics

- E-Textiles: Sensor-enabled clothing can track temperature, hydration, muscular activity, and heart rate.
- Athletes can receive real-time feedback from smart athletic wear, which helps them avoid injuries and perform better.
- Medical-Grade Smart Pajamas: Made to monitor

vital signs while you sleep, these pajamas are ideal for elderly and bedridden patients.

Injectable and Implantable Sensors

- Microchip Implants: Electrolyte, oxygen, and glucose levels can be tracked by tiny sensors inserted beneath the skin.
- Smart Pills: Real-time data on medicine absorption and gut health is transmitted by indigestible sensors.
- Neurotechnology Wearables: Brain-monitoring headbands identify neurological conditions like epilepsy and Alzheimer's early.

Insights into Personalized Health and AI Integration

- AI will be used more and more in wearables to offer personalized health advice.
- Using genetic information and lifestyle factors, sophisticated machine learning models will forecast the likelihood of developing certain diseases.
- Wearables and healthcare practitioners will be able to communicate easily thanks to integration with

electronic health records (EHRs).

By facilitating early diagnosis, individualized health management, and real-time disease monitoring, wearable health technology is quickly revolutionizing the healthcare sector. These gadgets, which range from biosensors and smartwatches to non-invasive glucose monitors and AI-powered cardiovascular tracking, are improving healthcare's accessibility and proactiveness.

A new era of customized medicine will be ushered in by future developments in wearable technology, including smart textiles, implanted sensors, and AI-driven health insights. As wearable technology develops further, it has the potential to lower healthcare expenses, enhance patient outcomes, and give people unprecedented control over their health.

CHAPTER 6

THE FUNCTION OF DNA SEQUENCING AND GENOMICS IN EARLY DETECTION

With their unmatched insights into disease risk, early identification, and viable therapies, genomics and DNA sequencing have completely transformed the medical industry. Healthcare practitioners can determine a person's susceptibility to certain ailments by deciphering their genetic code, which enables them to develop individualized treatment plans and preventative measures.

The potential for early disease identification and intervention is growing quickly with the introduction of next-generation sequencing (NGS) and gene-editing technologies like CRISPR. Alongside these developments, though, ethical issues pertaining to permission, privacy, and possible genetic information misuse must be carefully considered.

The core function of genomics in disease risk assessment, the revolutionary effects of next-generation sequencing, the promise of CRISPR to prevent genetic illnesses, and the moral ramifications of genetic testing are all covered in this chapter.

6.1 Learning About the Human Genome: How Genetics Affect the Risk of Disease

The human genome is made up of 23 chromosome pairs and roughly 3 billion base pairs of DNA. Variations in each person's genetic composition affect their vulnerability to certain diseases. Genetic mutations are the direct cause of many illnesses, but intricate interactions between genes and environmental factors are the cause of others.

Disease Susceptibility and Genetic Variants

1. The most prevalent genetic variations are called single nucleotide polymorphisms (SNPs), which can be used as indicators for illness risk.
   - Some SNPs are associated with a higher risk of developing diseases like diabetes, cancer, and

neurological disorders.

2. Monogenic vs. Polygenic Disorders:
- Monogenic Disorders: resulting from mutations in a single gene (e.g., Huntington's disease, sickle cell anemia, and cystic fibrosis).
- Multiple genetic differences combined with environmental and lifestyle factors can result in polygenic disorders, such as Alzheimer's disease, heart disease, and type 2 diabetes.

3. Epigenetics and Gene Expression:
- Epigenetic changes, including histone and DNA methylation, control gene activity without changing the DNA sequence.
- Diet, stress, and exposure to toxins are examples of environmental factors that might affect epigenetic modifications and the onset of disease.

Predicting Diseases via Genetic Screening

- Predictive genetic testing*, which evaluates a person's risk for hereditary disorders, is made possible by advances in genomics.

- Carrier screening assists in identifying people who possess genetic mutations that may be inherited by their children.

- Whole-genome sequencing (WGS) and whole-exome sequencing (WES) offer thorough information about a person's genetic susceptibility to illnesses.

Targeted therapies and customized medicine are made possible by early intervention tactics made possible by an understanding of the human genome.

6.2 Next-Generation Sequencing (NGS): Revolutionizing Early Disease Identification

The revolutionary technology known as next-generation sequencing (NGS) has greatly increased DNA sequencing's speed, precision, and affordability. NGS enables the quick sequencing of whole genomes or specific disease-related areas, in contrast to conventional sequencing techniques that examine DNA slowly and laboriously.

The Operation of NGS

NGS entails splicing DNA into tiny pieces, sequencing them all at once, and then using computer algorithms to piece the genetic information back together. Researchers and medical professionals may now identify mutations with previously unheard-of accuracy because of these parallel sequencing capabilities.

NGS Uses in Early Disease Identification

1. Using next-generation sequencing (NGS), cancer-related genes like BRCA1 and BRCA2, which are connected to ovarian and breast cancer, can be mutated.

- By analyzing circulating tumor DNA (ctDNA) in the bloodstream, liquid biopsy techniques allow for early cancer identification without the need for invasive treatments.

2. As evidenced during the COVID-19 pandemic, NGS is essential for detecting and monitoring infections through Infectious Disease Surveillance:.

- Rapid viral genome sequencing aids in the creation

of vaccines and the control of outbreaks.

3. Rare Genetic Disorders: A single gene mutation is the cause of many uncommon disorders. NGS makes it easier to diagnose diseases including Rett syndrome, muscular dystrophy, and hereditary metabolic abnormalities.

4. Newborn and Prenatal Screening:

- In order to identify chromosomal abnormalities such Patau syndrome, Edwards syndrome, and Down syndrome, non-invasive prenatal testing (NIPT) employs next-generation sequencing (NGS).

- Genomic sequencing is used in newborn screening programs to find curable genetic abnormalities at an early age.

NGS improves patient outcomes and lowers the burden of disease by enabling proactive healthcare interventions through improved early detection capabilities.

6.3 Gene Editing and CRISPR: Possibilities to Prevent Genetic Disorders

The revolutionary gene-editing technique known as CRISPR (Clustered Regularly Interspaced Short Palindromic Repeats) enables accurate DNA alterations. Because of this technology, doctors can now fix mutations at the molecular level, opening up new treatment options for hereditary illnesses.

The Operation of CRISPR

- A guide RNA (gRNA) is used by CRISPR to target a particular DNA sequence.
- The Cas9 enzyme cuts the DNA where it is wanted to by acting like molecular scissors.
- After the cut is repaired by the cell's natural healing processes, gene correction, deletion, or insertion is possible.

Potential Uses in the Prevention of Disease

1. Eliminating Genetic Disorders: In experimental settings, CRISPR has been utilized to fix mutations linked to Duchenne muscular dystrophy, sickle cell anemia, and cystic fibrosis.

- Early-stage studies point to the possibility of long-term remedies for hereditary illnesses.

2. Cancer Therapy:

- Gene editing can improve immune cells' ability to recognize and eliminate malignant cells (e.g., CAR-T cell therapy).
- CRISPR is being investigated as a way to fix tumor-suppressor genes or turn off oncogenes.

3. Viral Disease Resistance:

- Researchers are looking into whether CRISPR may eradicate latent viral illnesses like hepatitis B and HIV.
- By altering host genes that viruses take advantage of, gene editing may provide disease resistance.

4. Preventing Inherited Conditions in Embryos: Germline editing may be able to stop genetic illnesses from being passed along. However, its use in human embryos is restricted due to ethical and safety issues.

CRISPR has great potential to prevent genetic illnesses, but because of ethical concerns and possible off-target effects, its clinical application needs to be done carefully.

6.4 Genetic Testing Ethics: Consent, Privacy, and Possible Abuse

Concerns regarding data security, privacy, and the exploitation of genetic information have surfaced as genetic testing has become more widely available. To guarantee the proper use of genetic technology, ethical issues must be taken into account.

Important Ethical Considerations for Genetic Testing

1. Privacy and Data Security:
   - Genetic data includes extremely private information about a person's ancestry and health concerns.
   - The possibility of genetic data being exploited by employers, insurance, or unapproved third parties is increasing.

2. Informed Consent:
   - People who are getting genetic testing need to be

fully aware of the possible psychological and health effects.

- Unexpected information, including non-paternity or unreported familial disorders, may be disclosed by some DNA results.

3. Genetic Discrimination:

- People who are at a high risk of contracting an illness may be subject to discrimination from employers and insurance based on their genetic information.
- The goal of laws like the Genetic Information Nondiscrimination Act (GINA) is to shield people from this kind of prejudice.

4. Psychological Impact:

- Anxiety and emotional discomfort can arise when one discovers their hereditary susceptibility to certain diseases.
- To help people understand results and make wise healthcare decisions, genetic counseling is crucial.

5. Ethical Boundaries of Gene Editing:

- The possibility of designer kids and unforeseen genetic repercussions are concerns raised by germline editing.

- It is unknown how gene alterations will affect subsequent generations in the long run.

The Importance of Ethical Structures

- Regulations must be put in place to guarantee that genetic data is safely maintained and used only for approved purposes in order to address these ethical issues.

- Prior to doing genetic testing, obtain express consent.

- To help people comprehend the ramifications of their test results, offer genetic counseling.

- Provide precise rules for the moral application of gene-editing technology.

A new era of personalized medicine has been brought about by genomics and DNA sequencing, which have made it possible to identify diseases early, evaluate risks, and implement focused treatments. Even while technologies like CRISPR and NGS have a lot of potential to improve healthcare outcomes, ethical issues must come first to avoid abuse.

It will be crucial to strike a balance between creativity and moral obligation as genomic science develops to make sure that these potent instruments are applied for the good of humanity.

CHAPTER 7

ADVANCES IN AI-POWERED MEDICAL IMAGING AND RADIOLOGY

Artificial intelligence (AI) developments have transformed radiology and medical imaging, greatly enhancing the identification, diagnosis, and management of a wide range of illnesses. Artificial Intelligence has improved radiological evaluation accuracy, speed, and accessibility by utilizing deep learning algorithms and advanced imaging techniques. This chapter explores the ways AI is changing medical imaging, how it can be used to diagnose diseases early, and the technological and ethical issues that need to be resolved to fully realize its potential.

7.1 AI-Enhanced Medical Imaging using Deep Learning for Radiology

Radiology has been significantly impacted by deep learning, a kind of artificial intelligence that allows computers to evaluate medical images with previously unheard-of precision. In contrast to conventional rule-based systems, deep learning algorithms frequently outperform human radiologists in particular tasks by using neural networks to find patterns and anomalies in medical images.

Principal Ways AI Improves Radiology:

- Automated Image Analysis: AI-driven software can swiftly analyze vast amounts of medical photos and detect anomalies like lesions, cancers, or fractures. This lessens the possibility of human error and lightens the workload for radiologists.
- Improved identification of Subtle Abnormalities: Deep learning algorithms are able to identify subtle changes in tissues that the human eye could miss, increasing the likelihood of early illness identification.
- AI can evaluate complex scans in a matter of seconds, which speeds up diagnosis and allows for a quicker start to therapy.
- AI-driven radiology systems can be integrated with

patient records, cross-referencing imaging data with medical history to provide thorough diagnostic insights. This is known as Integration with Electronic Health Records (EHRs).

- Standardization of Interpretations: While radiological evaluations frequently differ amongst specialists, AI models use consistent analysis standards, which lowers diagnostic variability.

Notwithstanding these benefits, deep learning models need sizable, superior datasets in order to perform well. Before AI can be widely used in therapeutic settings, issues like algorithmic biases, a lack of data, and the requirement for regulatory permission must be resolved.

7.2 AI-Powered Prompt Identification of Brain Tumors, Lung Cancer, and Other Disorders

For diseases including cancer, neurological disorders, and cardiovascular issues, early identification is essential to increasing survival rates. AI has proven to be remarkably accurate at detecting diseases in their early stages, outperforming conventional techniques in this regard.

Early Disease Detection using AI Applications:

- Lung Cancer Detection: AI models trained on computed tomography (CT) scans and chest X-rays are able to identify lung nodules early on, allowing for prompt intervention. When compared to traditional radiologist ratings, Google's DeepMind and other AI-driven systems have demonstrated higher accuracy in lung cancer detection.

- Brain cancers can now be more accurately identified thanks to AI-assisted positron emission tomography (PET) and magnetic resonance imaging (MRI) scans. In addition to detecting tumors, AI can categorize them according to their aggressiveness and possible therapeutic avenues.

- The identification of breast cancer has improved due to AI-powered mammography interpretation, which has decreased false positives and needless biopsies. According to studies, AI can detect breast cancer in its early stages just as well as or better than human radiologists.

- Predicting Alzheimer's Disease: AI systems that examine brain scans are able to identify neurodegenerative markers long before symptoms appear, enabling early intervention techniques.

- Cardiovascular Disease Detection: AI-enhanced imaging methods aid in artery plaque detection, heart function evaluation, and cardiac event prediction.

The capacity of AI-driven early detection to offer a second opinion in complex instances is one of its most important advantages; it lowers the rate of misdiagnosis and guarantees that patients receive prompt and appropriate medical care.

7.3 Virtual biopsies and 3D imaging: non-invasive substitutes for conventional techniques

Conventional biopsies, which entail taking tissue samples for analysis, are intrusive procedures that come with risks of bleeding and infection. By providing non-invasive alternatives, AI-driven 3D imaging and virtual biopsy technologies are revolutionizing diagnosis.

3D Imaging Developments:

- Radiologists may analyze tissues more extensively thanks to AI-powered 3D imaging, which provides Higher Resolution and Greater clarity by reconstructing anatomical structures with remarkable clarity.
- Better Surgical Planning: By using 3D imaging to see intricate structures, surgeons can lower the danger of surgeries.
- Even in situations where low-quality scans would usually hide information, AI improves image quality through AI-Guided Image Reconstruction.

Virtual Biopsies' Promise:

AI-Based Tissue Characterization

- Without requiring physical biopsies, machine learning models evaluate imaging data to forecast the probability of tumor malignancy.
- Artificial intelligence (AI) algorithms improve functional magnetic resonance imaging (fMRI) and

PET scans by identifying alterations in cellular metabolism that signify the advancement of disease.

- Elimination of Unnecessary treatments: Virtual biopsies minimize patient discomfort by eliminating the need for expensive and difficult treatments.

Despite their ongoing development, these technologies mark a substantial advancement in medical diagnostics by lowering the need for invasive procedures while preserving accuracy.

7.4 Resolving Prejudice and Enhancing Precision in AI-Powered Radiology

Although AI in radiology offers a lot of promise, there are both technological and ethical issues. Algorithmic bias, which can result in differences in diagnosis and treatment recommendations, is one of the most urgent problems.

Difficulties and Moral Issues:

- Bias in Training Data: A lot of AI models are trained on datasets that aren't diverse, which makes underrepresented groups less accurate. AI systems that were predominantly trained on data from hospitals in the West, for instance, would find it difficult to analyze photos of patients in underdeveloped nations.

- Black Box Problem: Lack of Transparency" A lot of deep learning models function as "black boxes," which means that it is difficult to understand how they make decisions. When AI-generated diagnoses are inaccurate, this raises questions regarding accountability.

- Legal and Regulatory Issues: As AI becomes more prevalent in medical decision-making, concerns about liability in the event of an error or misdiagnosis surface.

- Ensuring Human Oversight AI should be used as an aid rather than as a substitute for radiologists. AI-generated insights are verified by seasoned experts when a human-in-the-loop approach is maintained.

Techniques to Increase AI Fairness and Accuracy:

- The ability of AI to perform accurately across a range of demographics can be improved by increasing the variety of training data.

- Explainable AI (XAI) Models: Creating AI systems that offer clear justification for their choices can increase healthcare professionals' trust.

- Regular Model Audits: To identify biases and inaccuracies, AI algorithms should be continuously assessed.

- AI and Radiologists Working Together: The greatest diagnostic results are obtained when AI's analytical capabilities are combined with human knowledge.

AI-powered radiography can deliver on its promise of offering high-quality, equitable healthcare to a variety of people by tackling these issues.

AI is revolutionizing radiology and medical imaging by providing previously unheard-of gains in illness detection, diagnostic precision, and non-invasive substitutes for conventional techniques. By automating picture analysis and identifying minute anomalies that human radiologists might overlook, deep learning improves radiological evaluations. AI-powered early detection has demonstrated significant potential in detecting diseases like cardiovascular disorders, brain tumors, and lung cancer.

The future of non-invasive diagnostics lies on 3D imaging and virtual biopsies, which improve accuracy while lowering the need for intrusive, expensive treatments. However, issues with prejudice, transparency, and ethical considerations must be addressed as AI continues to be incorporated into healthcare.

Going forward, cooperation between technology developers, healthcare providers, and regulatory agencies will be essential to the successful integration of AI in radiology. AI has the ability to completely transform medical imaging by guaranteeing accuracy, fairness, and human oversight. This would eventually improve patient outcomes and influence the direction of precision medicine in the future.

CHAPTER 8

POINT-OF-CARE TESTING WITH SMART LAB-ON-A-CHIP DEVICES

Large, centralized labs with highly skilled staff and advanced equipment have long been the mainstay of medical diagnostics. However, point-of-care testing has been transformed by the advent of Lab-on-a-Chip (LoC) devices, which allow for quick, precise, and affordable diagnostics in small, portable formats. Real-time health monitoring, biomarker analysis, and rapid illness diagnosis are made possible by these miniature diagnostic systems, which combine several laboratory operations onto a single microfluidic chip.

The basic ideas of Lab-on-a-Chip devices are examined in this chapter, along with their various uses in illness detection, their contribution to increasing access to healthcare in low-resource environments, and the prospects for AI-driven developments in this area.

8.1 Lab-on-a-Chip Devices: What Are They? Reducing the Size of Diagnostics

Lab-on-a-By combining microfluidics, biochemistry, and electronics, chip technology makes it possible to carry out laboratory procedures like DNA sequencing, blood analysis, and pathogen detection on a microscale platform. By processing small fluid quantities (often microliters or nanoliters), these devices use miniaturization techniques, which eliminates the need for costly reagents and huge sample sizes.

Important Lab-on-a-Chip System Elements:

- The exact manipulation and transportation of biological fluids is made possible by Microfluidic Channels, which enable regulated reactions and analysis.
- Biosensors: Integrated biosensors convert chemical interactions into readable signals by detecting certain biological markers like proteins, nucleic acids, or infections.

- In order to transport and mix samples inside the chip for precise testing, tiny pumps and valves are necessary for fluid management.
- Diagnostic data can be read out quickly and sensitively using optical, electrochemical, or electrical detectors (sometimes known as "on-chip detectors").
- Data Processing Units: To interpret test results and provide data wirelessly to healthcare providers, certain sophisticated LoC devices use computational components.

Due to the substantial time and cost reductions brought about by the shrinking of diagnostic systems, Lab-on-a-Chip technologies are revolutionizing quick diagnostics, tailored treatment, and real-time health monitoring.

8.2 Uses in Neurological Disorders, Cancer, and Infectious Disease

Lab-on-a-Chip technology offers quick and accurate disease diagnostics that may be performed at the point of care, and it has many uses in several medical specialties.

1. Diagnosing Infectious Diseases

In order to stop epidemics, start early treatment, and lower death rates, infectious illness identification must happen quickly. In the detection of bacterial, viral, and parasite illnesses, LoC devices have shown excellent sensitivity and specificity.

- Using nasal swabs or saliva, LoC platforms have been created to identify influenza and SARS-CoV-2 viruses, providing results in less than an hour
- In rural or poor areas, portable LoC systems provide prompt detection of HIV and TB, guaranteeing prompt treatment commencement.
- Malaria and Dengue Fever: LoC technology aids in the more accurate diagnosis of mosquito-borne illnesses than conventional techniques by identifying particular antigens or DNA sequences.

2. Cancer Monitoring and Detection

In order to diagnose cancer, biopsy-based histopathology** is usually needed, which can be invasive and time-consuming. By looking for circulating tumor cells (CTCs), exosomes, and cancer-specific biomarkers in blood, urine, or saliva samples, LoC devices provide non-invasive alternatives.

- Early Cancer Detection: LoC devices improve survival rates by enabling early diagnosis by the detection of genetic mutations, proteins, or metabolites linked to cancer.
- Personalized Cancer Treatment: Certain LoC platforms examine tumor microenvironments and forecast the potential response of a patient's cancer to particular therapies.
- Continuous Monitoring: Real-time monitoring of patients receiving immunotherapy or chemotherapy enables dynamic treatment plan modifications.

3. Diagnostics of Neurological Disorders

Imaging methods like MRI or invasive cerebrospinal fluid (CSF) analysis are frequently used to diagnose neurological diseases. For neurological diagnostics, Lab-on-a-Chip devices offer a less invasive and more accessible alternative.

- Early diagnosis of Alzheimer's and Parkinson's disease is made possible by LoC systems' ability to identify biomarkers in blood or cerebrospinal fluid, such as tau and beta-amyloid proteins.
- Stroke and Traumatic Brain Injury (TBI): Quick biomarker identification with LoC devices aids in determining the extent of brain damage and directing prompt therapy choices.
- Multiple Sclerosis (MS): Early and more precise diagnosis of MS is made possible by the identification of certain autoantibodies in blood samples.

Lab-on-a-Chip technology is revolutionizing illness detection and treatment by allowing quick, accurate, and affordable diagnostics.

8.3 How These Tools Enhance Accessibility in Environments with Limited Resources

The ability of Lab-on-a-Chip devices to bridge the healthcare gap in low-resource settings with limited access to advanced laboratory equipment is one of its most important benefits.

Advantages for Remote and Low-Resource Areas:

- Minimum Sample and Reagent Requirements: LoC devices use tiny fluid volumes to function, which lowers the expenses related to costly reagents and sample gathering.
- The portability and ease of use of many LoC systems, which are handheld or battery-powered, enable medical professionals to perform diagnostics in rural clinics or field settings.
- Rapid Disease Detection: LoC devices provide real-time results, allowing for prompt medical intervention, in contrast to typical lab tests that require days or weeks.
- Cost-Effective Healthcare Solutions: LoC

technology dramatically lowers the cost of diagnostic testing by minimizing reliance on large hospital laboratories, making it available to economically disadvantaged people.

- A lot of contemporary LoC systems include the ability to transmit results wirelessly to medical experts, enabling remote diagnosis and consultation.

In sub-Saharan Africa, for instance, LoC-based HIV viral load testing has enhanced treatment monitoring and adherence, which has eventually lowered transmission rates and improved patient outcomes. In a similar vein, disease control initiatives have been accelerated in India and Southeast Asia by tuberculosis diagnosis using microfluidic chips.

Although Lab-on-a-Chip technology has demonstrated its worth in environments with limited resources, issues like scalability, price, and regulatory approvals still exist. Reaching broad acceptance will require resolving these problems.

8.4 Lab-on-a-Chip's Future: Including AI and Real-Time Analysis

In order to improve the precision, speed, and predictive power of these devices, AI-powered diagnostics and real-time analytics represent the next frontier in Lab-on-a-Chip development.

Improvements in LoC Technology Driven by AI:

- Diagnostic errors can be decreased by using AI algorithms to examine biological samples more correctly than humans can. This is known as "automated image and data analysis."
- LoC devices can forecast disease progression, treatment responses, and recurrence probabilities by the integration of machine learning algorithms.
- AI-enhanced LoC systems may enable patients to do at-home diagnostics with automated result interpretation through Self-Operating Testing Kits, hence eliminating the need for clinical visits.
- In order to continuously monitor health indicators like glucose levels, electrolyte balance, or cardiac

biomarkers, future LoC devices may sync with wearables.

- Blockchain technology could be used by AI-integrated LoC platforms to protect patient data and guarantee privacy in cloud-based diagnostics.

Difficulties and Prospects

- Scalability and Manufacturing Costs: For broad adoption, large-scale manufacturing of LoC devices must become more economical.
- Regulatory and Ethical Considerations: To guarantee the security, precision, and moral application of AI-integrated LoC systems, governments and healthcare institutions must set unambiguous regulations.

Effective patient management requires

- Interoperability with Healthcare Systems
- Standardizing LoC device outputs for smooth incorporation into current electronic health records (EHRs).

By offering quick, portable, and affordable testing

solutions for a range of medical specialties, Lab-on-a-Chip technologies are revolutionizing point-of-care diagnostics. Their use in diagnosing neurological disorders, cancer screening, and infectious illness detection demonstrates their enormous potential to transform healthcare.

LoC devices provide a lifeline for underserved populations in low-resource settings, lowering dependency on centralized laboratories and increasing access to critical diagnostics. The capabilities of these smart diagnostic platforms will be further enhanced by the integration of AI, real-time data analytics, and wearable technology.

LoC technology's influence on the future of personalized, decentralized, and AI-powered healthcare will only grow as researchers continue to improve it. The upcoming ten years hold the potential for groundbreaking innovations that could revolutionize medical diagnostics and democratize access to high-quality healthcare globally.

CHAPTER 9

PREDICTIVE ANALYTICS AND PERSONALIZED MEDICINE'S FUTURE

9.1 Personalized Healthcare Is Emerging: Going Beyond One-Size-Fits-All

Conventional healthcare has long used a uniform, one-size-fits-all strategy in which drugs and therapies are created for the typical patient rather than for each person's unique needs. But thanks to developments in genomics, AI, and data analytics, healthcare is moving toward a more individualized strategy that optimizes treatment results by taking into account a patient's genetic composition, lifestyle, and surroundings.

The following are the main forces behind personalized medicine:

- Genomic and Molecular Profiling: By sequencing a person's genome, doctors can learn about drug reactions, illness risks, and possible treatment strategies based on genetic differences.

- Biomarker Discovery: Finding certain biological markers aids in prognosis, early illness identification, and tailored treatments, especially for ailments like cardiovascular disease and cancer.

- In order to provide predictive insights, provide treatment alternatives, and customize medication regimens based on patient-specific data, AI-powered algorithms may evaluate large datasets.

- Wearable and Remote Monitoring Devices: Vital signs can be continuously monitored with smartwatches, biosensors, and mobile health apps, enabling real-time, individualized health interventions.

- The field of pharmacogenomics: In order to help clinicians choose medications with the maximum efficacy and the lowest risk of side responses, this discipline looks into how a person's genes affect how they respond to drugs.

The emergence of tailored healthcare is changing the way that illnesses are identified and managed, turning medicine from a reactive to a proactive field. Clinicians can utilize genetic and biochemical data to predict risks and put preventive measures in place that are specific to each patient rather than waiting for symptoms to appear.

9.2 Predictive Analytics: Recognizing Patients at High Risk Before Symptoms Emerge

Using big data, machine learning, and statistical modeling, predictive analytics is revolutionizing modern medicine by predicting the course of diseases, identifying individuals who are at risk, and allocating healthcare resources as efficiently as possible. Predictive models can identify early warning indicators of a number of medical illnesses before symptoms appear by examining trends in lab results, imaging scans, wearable device data, and electronic health information.

Healthcare Applications of Predictive Analytics:

- Early Disease Detection: AI-powered models examine genetic predispositions, biomarkers, and patient history to forecast the risk of acquiring diseases including diabetes, cardiovascular disease, and neurological disorders.

- Risk Stratification: To prioritize high-risk patients and enable early interventions, hospitals employ predictive analytics to classify patients according to their risk levels.

- Hospital Readmission Prevention: By identifying patients who are likely to be readmitted after being discharged, predictive algorithms allow for proactive follow-up care and lower medical expenses.

- Sepsis and Infection Prediction: AI systems examine lab data and vital signs to identify early indicators of infections or sepsis, enabling fast medical treatment.

- Mental Health Predictions: Machine learning algorithms assess social media activity, speech patterns, and behavioral shifts to forecast suicidal thoughts, depression, or anxiety.

By facilitating prompt interventions, the incorporation of predictive analytics into standard healthcare not only improves early diagnosis but also patient outcomes. These models are being used by hospitals and clinics more and more to streamline operations, cut down on ER visits, and improve overall healthcare effectiveness.

9.3 Using AI to Integrate Electronic Health Records (EHR) for More Intelligent Diagnosis

Medical data management has been transformed by Electronic Health Records (EHR), but when AI is integrated with EHR, its full potential is seen. EHR systems with AI capabilities can uncover patterns in disease, draw insightful conclusions from patient histories, and assist clinicians in making decisions with previously unheard-of precision.

The following are some advantages of AI-integrated EHR systems:

- Automated Data Processing: AI can reduce the administrative load on healthcare personnel by extracting pertinent information from unstructured clinical notes, pathology reports, and radiology pictures.

- Clinical Decision Support: Artificial intelligence systems examine patient data to identify probable drug interactions, prescribe treatment regimens, and make potential diagnoses.

- Personalized Treatment Plans: AI can provide treatment alternatives that are specific to a patient's condition by comparing their medical records with extensive datasets.

- Artificial Intelligence (AI) identifies irregularities in billing records, preventing insurance fraud and guaranteeing adherence to legal requirements.

- Enhanced Patient Engagement: AI-driven chatbots and virtual health assistants give patients access to real-time health information, medication adherence assistance, and appointment reminders.

The potential of AI to identify tiny trends that human doctors might miss is one of the most promising uses of AI in EHR. AI can, for instance, use voice analysis to find hidden symptoms of neurological illnesses or analyze thousands of chest X-rays to find early-stage lung disease. AI integration in EHR will greatly increase diagnostic precision, lower medical mistakes, and boost healthcare delivery efficiency as it develops.

9.4 How Secure Data Sharing and Blockchain Can Enhance Early Detection Systems

Data security and privacy are now major issues due to the increased use of digital health records and predictive analytics. A decentralized, impenetrable system for safely storing and exchanging medical data is provided by blockchain technology, guaranteeing the protection of private health information and facilitating smooth interoperability between healthcare networks.

The following are some of the main benefits of blockchain technology in the healthcare industry:

- Enhanced Data Security: Blockchain encrypts patient records, lowering the possibility of cyberattacks and preventing unwanted access.
- Interoperability: Blockchain facilitates safe data exchange between wearable device manufacturers, hospitals, clinics, and research institutes by establishing a single, decentralized ledger.
- Patients are in complete control of their medical records and can designate particular healthcare providers as needed. This is known as patient-centric

data ownership.

- Immutable Medical Records: The integrity of medical histories and diagnostic results is guaranteed since data cannot be changed or removed once it is stored on the blockchain.

- Simplified Clinical Experiments: Blockchain improves cooperation between pharmaceutical companies, regulatory bodies, and healthcare providers by facilitating transparent data sharing in clinical studies.

Use Cases in Early Disease Detection:

- Secure Genomic Data Sharing: Blockchain speeds up the identification of genetic markers for diseases by allowing researchers to safely access anonymized genomic data.

- Predictive analytics can be improved by using decentralized AI training, which allows AI models to be trained on encrypted medical data without disclosing patient identities.

- Remote monitoring and telemedicine: Blockchain guarantees that health information from wearable technology and telehealth platforms is kept confidential and available to authorized personnel only.

Blockchain has the potential to completely transform the way medical data is stored, accessed, and evaluated as its use in the industry grows. Healthcare practitioners may create more dependable early detection systems that enhance patient outcomes and promote precision medicine by fusing predictive analytics with safe data-sharing methods.

AI, genomics, and safe data-sharing technologies are driving a more individualized, data-driven, and predictive approach to healthcare in the future. Instead of using a generic strategy, personalized medicine makes sure that therapies are customized for each patient. Early intervention is made possible by predictive analytics, which detects high-risk patients before symptoms manifest. AI-powered EHR systems improve diagnostic precision, expedite clinical procedures, and provide doctors with useful information. Blockchain technology, meanwhile, facilitates smooth interoperability between healthcare organizations while protecting patient data.

These technologies will completely change the healthcare industry as they develop further, increasing the accessibility and effectiveness of predictive healthcare, individualized treatment regimens, and early disease identification. The future of medical research, diagnosis, and treatment plans will be completely transformed by the combination of AI, big data, and blockchain. This will also lead to better patient outcomes.

CHAPTER 10

GETTING PAST ADOPTION OBSTACLES AND GUARANTEEING WORLDWIDE ACCESS

Global healthcare could be revolutionized by the development of medical diagnostics, especially in the area of early disease identification. But despite advancements in technology, major obstacles stand in the way of general accessibility and use. Innovative ideas need to be accessible, properly regulated, incorporated into healthcare systems, and backed by medical education and public awareness. To guarantee that people all throughout the world benefit from life-saving diagnostic tools, these issues must be resolved.

10.1 Cost and Affordability: Enabling Everyone to Access Cutting-Edge Diagnostics

Cost is one of the main barriers preventing modern diagnostic technology from being widely used. Even though technologies like liquid biopsies, lab-on-a-chip devices, and AI-powered imaging have shown remarkable potential, their high cost restricts accessibility, especially in areas with limited resources and poor incomes.

Main Cost-Related Issues:

- High Research and Development (R&D) Expenses: New medical technologies are expensive to create, test, and refine, which makes their initial market costs unaffordable.

- Advanced diagnostics frequently necessitate specific materials, cleanroom settings, and highly skilled staff, which raises production costs.

- Limited Insurance and Reimbursement Coverage: Patients must pay out of pocket for innovative diagnostic equipment because many insurance companies and healthcare systems do not now cover them.

- The cost of infrastructure in low-resource settings can be high since many new diagnostics require educated workers, cold-chain storage, or expensive laboratories, all of which may not be available in underserved areas.

Potential Solutions to Improve Affordability:

- Public-Private Partnerships: Governments, private investors, and non-governmental organizations (NGOs) might work together to finance research and production expenses as one way to increase affordability.

- Economies of Scale: As diagnostic tool adoption rises, mass production can drastically lower the cost per unit.

- Open-Source and Low-Cost Alternatives: Devices can be made more affordable by promoting open-source diagnostic solutions and utilizing 3D printing or microfluidic technology.

- By combining diagnostics with telemedicine, unnecessary in-person visits can be avoided, which lowers overall healthcare expenses.

- Insurance and Policy Reform: Promoting government financing and insurance reimbursement can increase access to modern diagnostics for a larger population.

Future developments must prioritize affordability to

guarantee that state-of-the-art diagnostic instruments are not only accessible but also financially viable for all healthcare systems, irrespective of socioeconomic background.

10.2 Regulatory Obstacles: Global Approval Procedures, FDA, and CE Marking

One of the most important and time-consuming obstacles to the implementation of novel diagnostic technology is regulatory approval. To guarantee the safety, effectiveness, and dependability of medical equipment, governments and international organizations impose stringent rules; nonetheless, these procedures sometimes cause delays and inconsistencies across various locations.

Major Regulatory Bodies:
- Prior to licensing novel diagnostic devices, the U.S. Food and Drug Administration (FDA) requires thorough clinical trials and evidence-based evaluations.
- The European CE Mark guarantees adherence to safety, health, and environmental regulations set

forth by the European Union (EU).

- Medical device approvals in China are governed by the National Medical Products Administration (NMPA), which has different regulations than those of the FDA and the EU.

- The World Health Organization's (WHO) Prequalification Program helps low- and middle-income nations approve diagnostics.

Main Regulatory Obstacles:

- Long permission Timelines: Getting regulatory permission can take years, which delays access to technologies that can save lives.

- Different Regional Standards: Manufacturers must adhere to several sets of regulations due to discrepancies between FDA, CE, and other regulatory bodies.

- Data Privacy and Compliance Issues: AI-driven diagnostics that depend on patient data sharing are impacted by stricter data laws, such as the GDPR in Europe.

- Balancing Innovation with Safety: Excessive bureaucracy can impede technological advancement, even while restrictions are required to maintain safety.

Methods for Simplifying Regulatory Approvals:

- Harmonization of Global Standards: Promoting the adoption of a single approval procedure by worldwide regulatory bodies would make it easier for innovative technology to enter the market.
- Regulatory Sandboxes: To expedite approval without sacrificing safety, certain governments have implemented "regulatory sandboxes" that permit real-world testing under controlled circumstances.
- Adaptive AI-Based Regulations: Regulators ought to create flexible frameworks that permit ongoing adjustments and enhancements, considering the dynamic character of AI-driven diagnostics.
- Fast-Track Approval for Critical Technologies: Urgent diagnostic advances could be subject to expedited procedures, akin to those utilized for COVID-19 vaccines.

In order to avoid needless delays and uphold strict safety and effectiveness standards, regulatory barriers must change in tandem with technology improvements.

10.3 Closing the Knowledge Gap via Medical Education and Public Awareness

Making sure that patients and healthcare professionals are aware of and adequately trained to use new diagnostic technologies is a major difficulty that persists even after they are authorized and made available. Lack of knowledge and awareness is the reason why many promising diagnostic innovations fall flat.

Difficulties in Medical and Public Awareness:

- Limited Knowledge Among Healthcare Providers: Underutilization of emerging diagnostic technologies may result from physicians, nurses, and laboratory technicians' unfamiliarity with them.
- Patient Skepticism or Mistrust: Many people may be skeptical of new technology because they are worried about privacy, cost, or accuracy, especially in communities where healthcare inequities have historically occurred.
- In the absence of standardized training programs,

healthcare professionals may find it difficult to incorporate new diagnostics into their practice.

- Digital Divide in Healthcare: Digital literacy is still a barrier in some areas, despite the rise of AI-driven diagnostics and telemedicine.

The following are some ways to raise awareness and enhance training:

- Medical Education Reform: Including new diagnostic tools in medical school curricula and ongoing professional development initiatives.
- Public Awareness Campaigns: To educate patients about the advantages of early detection technologies, governments and healthcare institutions should start educational programs.
- Telemedicine and E-Learning: Remote healthcare personnel can acquire the skills necessary to apply modern diagnoses through online training programs.
- The World Medical Association (WMA) and the American Medical Association (AMA) are two organizations that can assist in standardizing diagnostic training.
- Community-Based Outreach: Collaborating with

nearby health facilities and non-governmental organizations to inform people in underprivileged areas about the advantages of early detection.

Healthcare systems can close the gap between invention and real-world application by giving education and outreach first priority. This will guarantee that new technologies are successfully incorporated into routine medical practice.

10.4 What must occur in order for tech-driven early detection to become the standard

Coordination between several sectors, including healthcare, technology, policy, and education, is necessary for the broad implementation of technology-driven early detection. Even though there has been a lot of progress, a few crucial advancements are still required for these ideas to become widely accepted.

Key Steps for the Future:

- Expansion of Public and Private Funding: To make early detection technologies generally accessible, more money must be invested in diagnostics R&D, production, and distribution.

- Simplifying approval procedures, cutting down on red tape, and guaranteeing quicker market access for cutting-edge diagnostic technologies are all examples of regulatory modernization.

- Equitable Access Policies: Through nonprofit distribution models or subsidies, governments and non-profit organizations must guarantee that low-income and distant communities have access to life-saving diagnoses.

- Integration into National Healthcare Systems: To guarantee uniform usage of new diagnostic technologies in clinics and hospitals, they must be smoothly integrated into established medical procedures.

- Ongoing Developments in AI and Big Data: Data-driven diagnostics will become increasingly important in medical decision-making as their accuracy and efficiency increase.

- Ethical and Secure Data Handling: As AI and data analytics become more and more important, strong cybersecurity and privacy procedures need to be put in place to safeguard patient data.

The ultimate objective is to make sure that advancements in medical technology result in tangible benefits in patient outcomes. Collaboration between scientists, physicians, legislators, and the international community is necessary to realize this aim. Technology-driven early detection has the potential to become the norm, lowering the burden of disease and saving lives all around the world, with the correct funding, regulations, and education.

ABOUT THE AUTHOR

 Author and thought leader in the IT field Taylor Royce is well known. He has a two-decade career and is an expert at tech trend analysis and forecasting, which enables a wide audience to understand complicated concepts.

Royce's considerable involvement in the IT industry stemmed from his passion with technology, which he developed during his computer science studies. He has extensive knowledge of the industry because of his experience in both software development and strategic consulting.

Known for his research and lucidity, he has written multiple best-selling books and contributed to esteemed tech periodicals. Translations of Royce's books throughout the world demonstrate his impact.

Royce is a well-known authority on emerging technologies and their effects on society, frequently requested as a speaker at international conferences and as a guest on tech podcasts. He promotes the development of ethical technology, emphasizing problems like data privacy and the digital divide.

In addition, with a focus on sustainable industry growth, Royce mentors upcoming tech experts and supports IT education projects. Taylor Royce is well known for his ability to combine analytical thinking with technical know-how. He sees a time when technology will ethically benefit humanity.

www.ingramcontent.com/pod-product-compliance
Lightning Source LLC
LaVergne TN
LVHW051659050326
832903LV00032B/3912